SHEARSMAN
109 & 110

WINTER 2016 / 2017

EDITOR
TONY FRAZER

Shearsman magazine is published in the United Kingdom by
Shearsman Books Ltd
50 Westons Hill Drive | Emersons Green | BRISTOL BS16 7DF

Registered office: 30-31 St James Place, Mangotsfield, Bristol BS16 9JB
(this address not for correspondence)

www. shearsman.com

ISBN 978-1-84861-491-8
ISSN 0260-8049

Subscriptions and single copies

Current subscriptions—covering two double-issues, with an average length of
108 pages—cost £16 for delivery to U.K. addresses, £18 for the rest of Europe
(including the Republic of Ireland), and £21 for the rest of the world. Longer sub-
scriptions may be had for a pro-rata higher payment. North American customers
will find that buying single copies from online retailers in the U.S.A. will often be
cheaper than subscribing. This is because airmail postage rates in the U.K. have
risen rapidly, whereas copies of the magazine are printed in the U.S.A. to meet
demand from online retailers there, and thus avoid the transatlantic mail.

Back issues from n° 63 onwards (uniform with this issue) cost £8.95 / $16 through
retail outlets. Single copies can be ordered for £8.95 direct from the press, post-free
within the U.K., through the Shearsman Books online store, or from any bookshop.
Issues of the previous pamphlet-style version of the magazine, from
n° 1 to n° 62, may be had for £3 each, direct from the press, where copies are
still available, but contact us for a quote for a full, or partial, run.

Submissions

Shearsman operates a submissions-window system, whereby submissions are only
accepted during the months of March and September, when selections are
made for the October and April issues, respectively. Submissions may be sent
by mail or email, but email attachments—other than PDFs—are not accepted.
We aim to respond within 3 months of the window's closure, i.e. all who submit
should hear by the end of June or December, although for recent issues
we have often taken a month longer.

Contents

Ken Bolton

Fewer Pages—A Review

Fewer pages left—
in this pad I found—
than I thought.

Not a metaphor.

"(W)e've come to put our trust in suspicion"

says a canny review
in—the *London Review of Books*—

accurately shafting Alex Katz's innocence,
his having (finally, it becomes clear)

bitten off less than he might have chewed.

I like him—but agree.
I wonder if—like him—I have, too.

I always liked Katz. Tho it was clear
—*was it, always?*—they were not quite enough. The
emptiness was… "a little empty".

Bored, rich, the shirts too clean & pressed
(too 'Beach Boys–Pat Boone')—

characters preppy, bland,
unashamed, too—

a quality, this,
they held positively—

derived, says the reviewer,
from Manet &—further back, Velázquez—

or Milton Avery (a possible first instance)?

Now they *were* empty
(the Milton Avery)—

tho the colour might
also have been of note,

to Katz—a tip, an influence?

The books I'm reading, for various
reasons all halfway thru

—Sloterdijk, Roussel—one too
thoughtful for my current mood—

the other hard to read
except in the best light, *but funny*.

Susan Sontag I could pick up—
her journal, the second volume—

& drift back to the sixties,

my seventies. That is, 'the sixties' occupied
my *nineteen*-seventies.

Pam's recommendation—*Panegyric*—
at work,
where I take it
& read at lunchtime:
so amusingly declarative &
calculatedly 'insolent', harsh, firm,
cheerful (cheerful 'in despite'
of things).

Not very Alex Katz.

Too Gallic for the *London Review
of Books.*

   A snotty reviewer
damns Zadie Smith for
—pointlessly, he says—
focusing on guilt
at achieving a degree
of middle-class status. (Hard
to please the *London Review.*)

And then he ends: *Still, it
may be her best book.*
     'Take that'?

I sit with Pola for a bit.
Her doggy head absorbs a great deal
of massage & scrunching & stroking.

She rests it on her white paws,
wet, I see, from wading in the pool,
which she does
every so often, because it's there.

It might behove, or complicate
a Katz character,

but I don't want her to feel guilty. (Do *they*?
Katz's characters?)

The fish pond
is an amenity
she should use.
    How she sees it.

And we are amused.

And I write this…

because I can
& have time, suddenly, free—
a review written—that I dreaded—
days early!—
                    a busy week
thus prepped,
so my day off becomes
my 'day off', &, like a Katz character,
what to do with it?
Like Debord, sharpen
an axe or two?
Or like Manet—whose
Sunday sailors
sometimes were given
to wearing striped shirts,
straw hats—& hung, for comfort,
with the picnic basket

(but his 'Impressionist phase'—yes?—
he probably affected the carelessness.)

(Or not: must Manet
be *Oskar Kokoschka*? No,
much as I like Oskar K.)

One prefers the anxiety
of the woman & daughter,
near the train at the Gare St Lazare:

more stripes, but anxiety
in buckets.
                    #
              "One prefers"—
& I am *one* with that one.
How about you, reader?
                    #

Guy.

I heard an awful story once—
from the Children's Court
or Family Law—the judge asks,
And what is the child's name?
Gooey, comes the response.
Gooey? Yes, your honour.
How do you spell that? G. U. Y.
Judge nods.

Like the *London Review of Books*
I wonder—well, I might—how
did I get so middle class? And
how middle class, exactly (rather upper,
rather lower?) & how do I feel
about it?

Though I do not wonder.

                    The defining
middle class anxiety
might be
about becoming *no longer
middle class—losing the money.*
I will find out when I quit work:
A life not devoid of surprises.

I am not middle class enough,
for the *London Review of Books.*

Only an *Australian* this poor
would buy it. That's a thought.

(In England I would
'know my place'?

Ha ha.) In fact, I 'scarcely' buy it:

they write, begging for money.
Pam gets me a free, 'guest', or
'trial' subscription & they write
testily to her
that their gift subscriptions
are *not for* repeat
but for new *readers*: they have
seen through "Ken Dark Horsey"—
tho they "will *"honor
the subscription"*.

Another offer from them—
is addressed to me as Fran Daddo.
But I refuse, as Fran, to subscribe.
I plan to join next,
via Pam,
as Kenneth D'Accorsi.
Will my luck hold?

       The current issue—just when
I am about to throw it out—

suddenly becomes interesting.

"You think it's lame
& *then it isn't.*"

My ideas about Katz
shift and settle slightly—

I remember the extreme,
bleak serenity of some—

a wow factor associated
with Abstract Art—the paint

"as good as it is in the can".

Frank Stella? I remember
the intake of breath,

the Katz blues, the reds—like
gifts.

(Like compensation for the
emptiness—which they ask us to understand.)

(Sad, troubled pretty pictures.)

Jill Jones

About the Soul

Every isthmus is an opportunity,
every mouse is a rodent.
This is only the beginning.
Then the thugs arrive
and start dividing the factories.

Wires change direction.
What now?
The serious stuff goes underground.
That's some claustrophobia.

I've been calculated. I am a mix.
The brewing storm.
The churning soul.
Lace panties. All the fashion.

The thugs storm the soul.
I flee the isthmus in a skip.
The mouse builds its house
of lace. It seems to be
the better deal. Thank you.

My feelings saunter. I am arcades.
I fend for necessities.
The tiles are like fancies.
Ah, little beauty sounds
coming and leaving.

Two seconds into terrible
awe, then there's trouble.
But above, the blue west
chortles with bells.
It's the thing we need.

Fresh words
in itchy machines.

Accounting

As if aplomb was a value.
As if outcomes went anywhere.
As if shadows were made of more or less.
As if shadows were made.
As if there's nothing more precious
than light on earth.
Even sleep maintains this.
Who rests may not sleep.
Who sleeps may never rest
upon the dearest ground.

But how will you ever identify
these things if they lie untasted, if they
do not rattle or move, if they aren't said
among people. Therein lies a bond.
Therein lies a way beyond marks.

If the people will have you.
If history will jump. If epochs will gape.
If laws will succumb, if not the years.

Because time is dumb, actuarial
seasonal, full of so much verve.
There's something more or less
blue in all this.
No wonder it's not to be trusted.

I want the yellow city.
I want some of the cold light as well.
But I want most of all
the living, that they live
without all the modest accounting.

If there are no exceptions, and this ground
is dangerous, you may learn
how to comprise yourself.

The Variances

looking for ways to write back losses
I camp out waiting for a verdict
yellow drips into me

                my left hand shakes uncontrollably
          some days find me with the lucky wafer
            a walk to the back fence can be long

high moon in late blue sky
only halfway coming into its sphere
petals shrivel eventually

                  everything smells of sap
                    the world is a vegetable
                    its pollen marks my sleeves

if exactitude is a virtue
my head spins
even the district seems insufficient

                  bird are crazy and click fences
             there's a warning attached to clouds
              it's precise if you can ever read it

rain scatters in minutes
and hours remain dry
the open garden is full of stories

                  my eyes haven't blown up
            heat sits all round like a fat chance
                I have medication forever

a position is like work
or a guest who pulls your life together
it becomes another question, doesn't it?

                everything must be examined
            though every day is simply a sample
              even if it falls, even as it fails

now I'm slippery like defeat
pressure is apparent in what doesn't happen
in one leap, one door knock, the click of officials
again, nothing happens
there, it's happening again
it's chancy, speculative, foolish
money ineffably shines
a guitar sings in an elevator
what is it about the sound of the room?
the amazing walls, the insects, the choir
what of crows in tender temperatures?
perhaps there are alternatives
go back into years and check the papers
in the world of reunions there's a world of grudges
weather catches on the window
like a horizon with a demand
a lure on the surface of the river
it's almost like dancing
it's still a passage of the real
time is less than time is more than
it isn't restitution but shorter than itself
as if we were adorned with numbers
as if sounds remembered this
the present seems to have passed
the pain in my shoulder remains
all the joins in the sentence
connect to the sun and the sky
air is variance, different fences, different acts
growth isn't simply a carnival
the next day things need to be done
tastes are never strange
they've passed me before
purpose freshens me up
sound is everywhere, in nests of dust
in the tentativeness of the sun
but where should I take the cold?
I bend down to listen, discarded hair sings
under canopies, kindness, shadows
a day quickens with darkness

Sheila Mannix

Baltimore in Twelve

One

The Postman speaks Latin. "*UBI SUNT,*" he cries, in a West-Country accent. A medievalist re-enacter, no doubt. I foresee dwells and laments on the transitory nature of life and beauty. "Where are they?" Where, indeed. "You said seventies bungalow. The place is full of seventies bungalows. You said palm trees. The place is full of palm trees." On the radio: howling like wolves at the side of the road...the dandelion verges on being a symbol...a wolf slaughtering a black lamb and Vulcan hovering over the scene...is there any such country? The herding of the cows lashed across the skies of Ireland. Durations, dynamics, articulations.

Two

Two magpies in the garden
Cordylines, dog-roses, wild
Sea grass with squid leaves

You could put that on a menu
Set up a stall in the market
And now for the good news!

Three

Excavate. Archaeology of Self. Yes, we've all read Lacan. I can still hear Emilia Weber's laconic, "Have I confessed something?" Let's start with the books. Sceptics, cynics, romantics, revolutionaries, hermits, beatniks, punks, dissidents, decadents, oulipians, existentialists, three waves of feminists, atheists, nihilists, idealists, materialists, anarchists, communists, socialists, realists, naturalists, abolitionists, expressionists, impressionists, symbolists, modernists, linguists, cubists, structuralists, satirists, classicists, formalists, futurists, constructivists, semiologists, dadaists, surrealists, absurdists, psychoanalysts, situationists, neo-realists, relativists, postmodernists, deconstructivists, liberationists, ecologists, vitalists, conceptualists, post-humanists, objectivists, phenomenologists, post-structuralists, neo-avant-gardists, trans-avant-gardists, post-avant-gardists, neo-modernists, post-postmodernists... I meant Dust. Forget I ever used the word *Evacuate*, I mean *Excavate*.

Four

Brief tableau.

FINNEUS *faces a wall and replicates imaginary death positions, wears a long black robe.* STONE *smokes and drinks wine, sports knuckle dusters under lace mittens.*

STONE: Let's give mystic nature a bash. For the competitions.

FINNEUS, *engaged in act of auto-asphyxiation, turns to* STONE.

STONE: Here goes. Storm-fronts queue dark skies like jets on a
    runway. A saffron-orange ferryboat is away to Cape Clear.

FINNEUS: I'm reluctant.

STONE: We're broke.

FINNEUS: We have enough to eat and a roof over our heads.

STONE: I'm running out of wine.

FINNEUS [*Sighs.*]: Beyond the Sound the islands Horse, Hare.

Five

A subject comes into being who has been mortified in his sovereignty, whose "crown" has slipped into the "creaturely." This subject has passed through an abjection and has constructed – through the "artifice" of material and mental writing and drawing – a new ego, a Lacanian sinthome, a dialogical self.

Six

STONE: More complications!

FINNEUS: Wasp's nest under eave. Wasps thud and whirr, destroy
    my ease. Buzz-off wasps. DIE!!!

STONE: What? Are you referring to me? You kill woodlice, fruit-
    flies, mice, rats. You're some Zen-Buddhist.

[FINNEUS *jumps up.*]

FINNEUS: Enough of this self-laceration! I cannot be a monk on
    a rock!

[FINNEUS *sets to ramble.* STONE *follows him.*]

STONE: Sage-green, duck-egg-blue. Palette of the bourgeois. Apt
    called Plantation shutters. What a beautiful view of the sea!

Seven
Pointillist Skittles: *An Fern Eile* or The Other Fern

At the cove, buoys bob "like a packet of Skittles," says Fern
– A pointillist sea, said Ella

White sails
Wings

Gulls
And
Boats

Echo
Each other

Dry-stone walls
Hedgerows of fire-grass, fuchsia: blossom, pre-historic fern

        H
        U
        M P
             B
          A
        CK

Hills.

Eight
Thorny. Yellow. Gorse. Tropics. Nose. Neon. Pink. Heather.

Nine
STONE: [*Back home with a French novel, types on laptop.*]: Finalement, on cherche l'exégèse en toute chose. Fuck's sake. Putting these symbols in. I can't see a thing. You've done the wrong one, you plonker.

Ten
The Postman is a mine of information. He says, "The old red sandstone grits have been altered in colour by the heat of the igneous

rocks, being white instead of red. The igneous rocks are greenstone, being both contemporaneous and intrusive. The old red sandstone is covered generally by carboniferous limestone. By far the larger part of the surface of Ireland consists of carboniferous limestone. The carboniferous slates have been formed of the products of the destruction of various older rocks. In the carboniferous rocks more than 500 species of fossil plants have been found, including ferns and gigantic clubmosses, also the wings of beetles, spiders, and other insects. There are numerous evidences of a glacial period when the northern hemisphere was subjected to a climate of the utmost rigour." I'm thinking Russian revolution, communists, 'greenstone' for Ireland, eco-warriors, movement of global capital, neo-liberal austerity. ...Anti-Oedipus: Capitalism and Schizophrenia, Postmodernism, or, the Cultural Logic of Late Capitalism. I'm hungry. What time is it?

Eleven

FINNEUS *picks magic mushrooms in the cliff-top pastures by the Baltimore Beacon. Blue skies and sunshine, the ocean sparkles.*
FINNEUS [*Sings*]: Beat up little seagull
          On a marble stair

          Trying to find the ocean
          Looking everywhere

          Hard times in the city
          In a hard town by the sea

          Ain't nowhere to run to
          There ain't nothing here for free

          Hooker on the corner
          Waiting for a train

          Drunk lying on the sidewalk
          Sleeping in the rain

          And the people hide their faces
          And they hide their eyes

'Cos the city is dying
And they don't know why

Oh, Baltimore
Ain't it hard just to live

Oh, Baltimore
Ain't it hard just to live
Just to live

Got my sister Sandy
And my little brother Ray

Buy a big old wagon
To haul us all away

Live out in the country
Where the mountain's high

Never gonna come back here
Till the day I die

Oh, Baltimore
Ain't it hard just to live

Oh, Baltimore
Ain't it hard just to live
Just to live

Twelve

The Baltimore Beacon is a white-painted stone beacon at the entrance to the harbour at Baltimore, County Cork, Ireland. The beacon was built at the order of the British government following the 1798 Rebellion. It was part of a series of lighthouses and beacons dotted around the Irish coast, forming a warning system.

'Baltimore' was composed by Randy Newman and originally appeared on his 1977 album *Little Criminals*.

Michael Farrell

The Artist

has four Arms and they are assumed to live
a sheltered Life. but an artist falls in love
with a Murderer, in love with the child
of a Murderer, in love with the brother
of a Murderer, in love with a suspect and
a Witness. the artist's barista is also murdered
this admittedly is Shelter, compared to the
Lives of those just mentioned. there is sweetness
out of Windows, but try to imagine a time
before Windows. everyone you see is painting
a Picture on a wall and when you go up close
You see it is their self portrait. some People are
alarming; sometimes the Artist is one of those
People. try and soothe them, try and find out
their favourite Tunes in order to soothe them
this is barbaric, You say, when you come across
their Writing in an email sent to an editor. the
Culture of barbarians is older than that of magazine
Editors, let alone emails, so respect that, please
if an Artist hurts you physically by all means
report Them: they are not above the law. they
contribute to the Law, but so do you. they have
four Arms to hit you with, but you have a lot of
Skin like everyone else, with nerve endings
You might pogo down the street and see a gang
beating up an Artist. use your pogo stick in any
way You feel comfortable in order to afford the
Artist protection. this need not be a violent use
be creative, if Anxiety doesn't override this
Possibility. anxiety can be used creatively if you
think for a Moment. time tends to slow down during
Acts of violence, and while this seems unfortunate
to the Victim, it can be vital for the use of the hero

this Time is similar to artistic time, but it reflects
a different Colour and it vibrates with a different
Sound. they have taken all the willows from the
River, wanting to free the river of the willows
Where else would such a thing happen? councils
are the same Everywhere. the artist follows the river
Track, stops at the bouquet of flowers signifying
Someone has drowned here. the artist moons, muses
for a while until a Family with dogs appears to
be heading in the same Direction. the artist wants
to be more at Ease with dogs but not today. the
Artist is in love with one who is in love with dogs

History of the Choo Choo Train

We all have parents dispersed throughout the world
I don't want to stand here with my arm in the door
like a Hawk waiting to catch a poet's eye. drip, drip
the Weather calls him. so much to be interested in
that's not a Street. do you live here, on the track?
not on the Track, sighed the snail, bleeding from its
gold Chain. at the last carriage, they're unloading
Cups of sugar, pans of rain; an occasional skeleton
for the Science lab. then it's off to collect the uniformed
Crims that mass waiting at the next station, many
with a toy Pigeon in a cage for effect. they dragged
my Breakfast out of the hill and killed a few miners
doing so, chuff-chuff. I've never handled a gun
Myself, though i once scared a horse with a sheet
of Roofing iron: that was depressing enough. histories
always remind Me of the great chewing gum drought
of '45. You can give me a bit of that gravel: i like
both Bum cheeks to be equally uncomfortable. my
Head swivels, scanning the hills for picturesque
Wells and cute carts. if only i'd watched that nightsoil
Documentary, i could describe the sight of the
Potato farmers as we pass them, grazing their dirt
with our cowlash Eyes. the train sighs: for its age

its Transgressions, its incomprehension, doubtless
it's like Everything is an artwork already: what use
Notebooks or canvas? each paddock like a blanket
the Cemeteries beg to be chess matches, anything
moving. it can't end with Everything covered in green
but rather a Hum and a raising of cabbage tree umbrellas
and in curious tough old Cows coming to the fence

Embrace a Rising Tide

I took four photos of your differences
by the Sea, overlooking *madame bovary*
on the Bed. there's quite a big fire, down
there by the Cliff but no one's taking any
notice, I guess it's all right then? this tuna
was caught by the Chef's father this morning
according to the Chef. a condom bookmark?
clean I hope – you should know. my head's
a Duck's from reading about community, the
Fishhook seems fresh at least. read or write
or take a Pill. sheets marked by books and
Salt spilling through the air. recount an
Opera that you saw. tell me why you play
that Song. you rode here on a bike and you'll
probably leave on One: your helmet appearing
through the Apertures in the white stone. look after
your Skin. there's sand in the coffee again, and
I just found out you're reading hemingway
with a Flaubert dust jacket! well, really
We both should modernise: read hazzard
or Malouf. hazzard: she's a friend of yours?
hardly a Friend, we met in cannes and i
mentioned the Rent and she gave me her
Villa for six months while she went to tibet
a friendly Action, and i loved that time
though I was always a bit nervous of having
Men there. a lot of men i mean. leaving marks
on the Walls and books … breaking things

Michael Ayres

Inside a book

Ten years inside a book. And all the things he encountered there
sustaining a kind of afterglow, happily forever after
blurred like the lights of a departing train
in a mid-summer shower, the very
last to leave the station tonight.
A great oversight, to set against a great fecundity.
Ogres, musicians, poets and pigs, and whole cities
hidden inside the bud of a rose:
magicians, psychos, sailors, populace enough to cast
a thousand Shakespeares, and sad palaces
sufficient to expel a million Versailles,
with mazes of mirrors innumerable
as the waves of the sea,
with their reflected jewels of images
like shimmering weapons drawn,
more than adequate to exhaust
a hundred years of glaziers' armouries.

And in that book, intense and detailed love.
Duels fought for honour in a mist-hushed meadow,
life stripped back to its essence and its end,
in the pulses of principals and seconds
the working parts revealed, the cover thrown open
on the relentless engine of moments.
Intense, and harrowing, and detailed love.
Engagements and derangements,
wild scarlet hullabaloos and deer-leap fleeting
visions on the run, in motels and mid-70s discos,
beds that become Africa or Antarctica,
with hipsters and youngsters, the fools and the wise
all equally desperate to read the signs
inside their hearts, to search for their kind of others,
at last to find themselves in their lovers' eyes,

and so, in the night shift, as always,
plenty of work for Saint Valentine.

And in that book, a cornucopia of locations,
from Mondrian uptown boogaloos of New York traffic,
to the golden boredom of the August steppes,
the simmering bullion of ripening grain
and too much Soyuz-blue space to entertain
lasting thoughts of rebellion.
A stream of concepts, too, and a glisten of dragonfly minds
flitting above them; and in the evening
the drifting fireflies of dreams
as if scattered from some distant conflagration.
Doors, and doors, and doors, and doors!
Such an opening and a closing, a clicking and a slamming shut
as might compose a staccato symphony,
each and every one the result of a vital decision.
Furore, tumult, gods and bores.
Episodes and incidents. Crescendos and interludes.
And sometimes, even, moments of pure peace.
An abrupt departure. Back-stories. Plot-holes.
The moral, supposedly.
The climax.

What was it like, the world he found
when he emerged at last from within that book?
Like Crusoe or Rip van Winkle,
Dracula hammered into his coffin, or Howard Hughes
tented in oxygen and dollars,
it had been a while.
Was it as he remembered? How had it changed?
With his butterfly beard and haze of reference,
what did he make of a planet returned,
the new schools, radical movements,
happening styles, deep cuts, fresh grooves?
When he heard the voices, did they make sense?
And had his opinion altered at all
on what appeared to happen
when words melted into silence?

The most wonderful production

"Will there be wolves in the forest?"

Of course! It wouldn't be a forest without wolves!
Snakes and bears, and ogres too no doubt.
My father's voice, like any voice,
partakes a little of what he talks about.
It carries the books, and lights the tiny lanterns
inside the grave. And my father tends to the snowflakes,
arranging them in the air, ensuring each one is a hexagon,
explaining to each their duties,
which must flutter, and which should drift.
My mother provides the sky.

I need a sky to roam beneath.
Wandering: that's my forte.
And my mother, being conscientious, appoints the sky with stars.
The moonlight gives off a spicy odour,
reminding me of Zanzibaran cinnamon floating on a frosty breeze
from the white direction of the Speicherstadt one winter.
Ah: and now — who's this? My brother!
Nettles: streams: whatever! He cuts a dash,
and with his sabre waves the wolves away.
I wanted them to creep closer.
To ask them if they remember Eden —
from the fervour of their stare,
I think they may do.

The books are dangerous.
Open, they lie, a landscape of exhausted mines,
and every now and then a person vanishes
underground as the earth subsides.
There are whole worlds inside those paper shafts.
Worlds of ivory and idiolects.
And of words pouring down like September birch leaves.
I am inside the vein with the forest,

searching for the exquisite musicians of insects
my father has put there, so the snakes have food.

I wander, and wander, and write down my thoughts.
I find there is a diminutive puzzle at the heart of each thing:
I call these moments. I never solve any.
My brother, of course, insists they are simple,
nothing to worry about at all.
I want to question him, but he only sounds his silver bugle,
and spurs on his charger, already eager for another war.
When he's gone,
his scarlet tunic, with the golden braid,
leaves no shape of him for me to hold.
I stroke the sleeves and the splendid buttons,
a special garment, yet one that seems to me, more or less
uniform with emptiness.
My mother calls.

My father calculates the sun away,
and dithers with the moon instead, just as normal;
he tinkers with the mechanism.
In a little while, I'm sure, it will be perfect.
My mother plays the piano, this evening Chopin is happy.
And in this way, the weightless continuum of my family
maintains its place on Earth.
In the ravines inside my bed, I feel
we have mounted the most wonderful production.
Even now, as my mother strokes my fringe
of sand-blond hair out of my gaze,
and I prepare to save the baby ogre
from the wrath of the ignorant villagers,
I feel the show will never end,
and as I close my eyes, hear my father's voice
tend the tiny lanterns inside the grave.

Julie Maclean

In the Annals of Tourism at The British Library

'But I don't want to go among mad people,'
–Lewis Carroll, *Alice's Adventures Under Ground*

Once I'd boned up on
Von Guérard and Buvelot,
Warhol just in case,
up to the armpits
in special facts, anecdotes highlighted in fluorescent pink,
jokes to break the ice
and readiness to say
'I don't know now,
but will find out' when asked 'Did Gauguin visit Geelong?'
it was not my job to measure satisfaction
although mine stood at zero
in a range of 1-10, ten being 'most satisfied'.
In a co-production there might
have been asides and a giggle,
light at the end of a worthy tunnel.
In its absence I conducted a 'probabilistic analysis
of guided tours during the slack season' and found that
guiding a tour on Saturday in regional Australia
is a waste of blood and adrenaline since most
of the population is doing the weekly
shop or yelling from the flanks of a foreign field.
Fanatics in pursuit of the pneumatic, he might have said,

or engaged in what is known as Aussie Rules—
the first and subsequent being fuck knows.
Maybe I should have devised
an 'alternate approach to modelling the slack
season provision of guided tours to tourists'
Tourist Management, Vol.31 (4) pp 482-485 (Peer reviewed)
Our slack season's been running for two hundred plus
non - peer - reviewed years.
Answer under my breath   No, you idiot!

Witches' Familiars

In the footprints of a small bat
consider   time-varying vortices,
the art of tracking a mate by its echo,
the business of sex before hibernation,
tucking sperm into a warm vestibule for spring.

From my glassy hallway one wobbled into my night light
more robust than a moth but confused
by the false forest, the disappointment of a house

shut and flat,
her furthest hands stroked the air in loops—

up and up, in and in   looking for hibiscus

to pollinate   a roosting tree, a sign.

In an abstract she alone transforms '… *modelling strategies
in the study of natural and manufactured
flying devices.*'

but of all her brilliances
it's those tiny incisors puncturing unsuspecting skin,
injecting a dose of Draculin to stop the clag
then lapping a teaspoon of blood.

It may seem macabre but if I wound my time-varying hands back
I'd have one for a pet and train her
to recognise the throb of a clotting brain

and marvel as she moved laser-quick

    to the strokes
        that separated hemispheres

        of my pre-disposed Nan
        with the task of returning words

        drowned in valleys,

        my forgotten face, her first song.

On Marriage and Misremembered Spectacles

In her quest for independence girl drives truck with workboot
hard on accelerator. Lime velour seat so far back she corrects
by groping for the lever. Upon arrival she remains outside
to witness the end in the guise of a wedding.

She's chosen the wrong plant, bamboo the size of a gorilla
when she should have selected the palm   several already
placed artfully around the pool with no fish.
People she knows wear red lipstick, even the men.

Most disappointing is the woman with bad teeth carrying a card
stating her intent to celebrate marriage in the official sense
but when asked how business is going says Terrible
due to her personality which is slight and those English teeth!

The girl is not looking for a man or a wedding.
Anyway, that dress reveals so much of the celebrant's breasts
and only the bride is allowed to do that. She goes back
many times having left so many clichés behind.

A briefcase, keys, a bicycle. It takes years to retrieve each one.
In the end she gets there in a blue Mini, bike in the boot,
seat in Stepford position. She finds her glasses in the
glove-box and thinks, What a quaint idea. Vroom.

Mark Goodwin

Ptarmigan Mist, Am Bodach, March 2016

Note: *Am Bodach* is a mountain just north of the head of Loch Leven;
its name means – *The Old Man.*

behind us is
sunlit snow

& soft white blades
of corniced ridges

& Am Bodach's
black rocks set

in shining névé

parts of our
minds are

behind us on
Am Bodach's

summit at a

recent past set
in a glistening

history of

lit minutes & iced
metres we have

just traversed

at summit fog
enfolded ground

and we descended
through grey air

on mist-smudged snow
and just to our

north the faint

dangerous line where
sky & cornice merge

and to south
clear black rocks

of safe solidity
up-poked and

marked way

now here in

a fog-hollow of
corrie in

front of
us perched on

a snow-tussock
a ptarmigan

bold & gazing
caped in white

red-smudged black
-slash eye-mask

hooked apple-pip beak
thick frosted legs

his

sudden ratchety
guttural call a

miniature thunder

he is

massive in his
little proudness

a bird of
mountain

his feathery
snow slopes his
crag-black rudder

his cornice-grace
ful curves

in front of us
now a mountain
of bird

set in mist pulls
Am Bodach's

mass and we
are tiny figures

climbing along a
ptarmigan's wing

Fox Caller

my brother blows his fox-lure

as sun slips away we crouch
in long grasses again

my brother blows his
rabbit-mimic a

high-pitched thin smear
of rabbity anguish vibrates

dusk's air and

again my brother blows so
              it seems a rabbit's voice

repeatedly cleaves

our old-home valley's
thickening darkness then

the breathy *hark*
of a fox-bark stretches

from hunger's or
fear's muzzle

to our
human ears

my brother shines
a quarter-mile

of torch beam and scrapes
pasture & hedgerows with

a tiny patch of day

the beam's dancing
          gnat-sparks seem

to soundlessly sing a gauze
of summer night and it's as

          if each
patch

of illuminated foliage is
a grey but gleaming

memory of
daylight's green growth

my brother swings the beam back
& forth through

night's swell

his scraping sweeps reveal
five foxes' gazes as

pairs of pale bright vibrating

planets hanging amongst
grasses & hawthorn leaves

another silvery trickling rabbit squeal

and across the valley (beyond
the brook) these watchful planets

          appear to pull

fox-shapes across the pasture
towards us but

                    no fox comes close

Tom Cowin

Bishopstone : Tidemills

downridge raised above a wash of dried
chalk foam   descend the uncropped

path as per guide   on foot turning
brittle carline thistle knots   the sum

is more hurt and walking grinds
the glass in the ankles   Ouse

estuary sump dragonflies jag
the reeds   the beaten zone

mocks natural landscape and the lives
moved from aggregate beach

you would ghost this coast more
than this haunting if I thought so

I try not   littoral hardcore
and concrete remains tide

resistant and footsore   keeping
defilade by sunblinding and being

elsewhere from reachable   past
the stationmaster's ruined walls

and wild mallow interiors
I am soled with sea beet leather

and hope against all that all
ordinance will fall at my feet.

FrostHeave

Waking the dominant cause of displacement
in frost morning heaving like whispers
under the eyes ice lenses so far removed
and amused they haunt loosening the soil
above the continual addition of days
and days such as these the startling
autonomous intrusion of angel-blank commuters
their stares all caution inclement and slippery
surface below the rime line of separation from miles
and miles of car dealerships as far as sight
we breathe eyelid soft clouds dissociate
water from light and long for another time.

Highland Poem

pylons make strange distance
pulled so taut a rhythm
the colour of storm threat

guardians of Sika
those black dogs of sight corners
would burn beyond ever

carrying electro magnetic
Gabriel Hounds wired across
the wet crackling land

over hydro thundering
hollow earth
below the cables slowly

recomposes distance becomes
memory at the point
of convergence in anode mud clouds

spreading below the radar
across the lines ringing
aeolian in the buzzard winds

Drying the shallots

Racked up and challenging
    for brightness
        the sunwhispering
through the slats
of the otherwise empty shed

sounds of the railway
    murmur under
        almost sacred shafts
of light and shadow geometries

slow full of dust whorl
a growth of unbreathed air
    the smell

is lachrymatory stillness
cut by a platform whistle

in air dry as light
    magenta flushed skin
and sun hungering
    green spears
become paper
    and straw   a syncope
        decay stalled
    his heart
manifest in the particular.

Stuart Cooke

Partial, & Remorse

—what we're left with here is a hand in another
(the close examination of a knuckle): what

happens now, what
happens now—these blurred
                            wrens darting

into the scrub
behind us—to us (in the wind

swept channel, the whipped
cream of a tide's top
                    retreating

                        the available possibilities in the tattlers
the gingery hind-leg of a
                        memory as it touches

an oyster catcher floating above the bow)—

back then (carving my lungs from the water)
when I clung to you

like a barnacle on a hull: gestation
of a muscle you didn't want

timbre of the flattest peaks;
                        circuit of the smallest wing—
what happens now, in your murky wake?

(as if the sky's searing slap:
winded in the thump, the delicious beasts

of the blue-
               green multi, their hooking
spoon) coughed spume
                              torn

and ionic, coming up for air (where are you?)
                              breaching that wary void

corrugated
               glimmers, the ecstatic
noun of a night's suffocated face, seated

                                             amongst bells:
                                             amongst hands

               my feet are eaten by a magma
slithering below the surface of the sand is
                                             needing

what I need, further & prior to any of this: your
relentless desire—the design
                              of a coast

one waiting for the other's
                              unwavering voyage

Black Rocks
Bundjalung National Park

coal bones of the old men
                    groan amongst the green
                              thrush the pools'
          little mouths wide open
                              & cedar calls
          from fuzzed black heads

               it's wallaby time, sea eagle time, it
                              steps
          into the onshore
                    to trace a law
                              between cliff & low
               tide I'm bounding

     off to fern country
thump
          & thud past charred
               mobiles swooning in the jade
                              spill
               our afternoon
                         glint the river shivers

     river glass
slices
          & sieves it roots
               relaxing into bank
                         all my feeding my
               loaming neither here
                         nor there there (whip

box) streaks
     & knots of
               cumulus over the low
          sun we swirl
               pearl

                    shell my plate
          python jaw waits
                              pity
          the mice the chicks
          the stroll tuned

to tuber & tubular trunks
     vibrate huge &
               not-so-sized the shrill
     the eagle keeps stretching the tide
          to the river creeping
                    behind the dunes we curl

their iridescent shadows
          until the change

Maria Jastrzębska

from The True Story of Cowboy Hat and Ingénue

Inside the truck there was almost no light except for the smallest crack in the metal shutter doors, which enabled her to guess if it was day or night. The drivers had shouted that they were not to try opening the doors when the truck stopped or they could be apprehended, maybe shot. They had stopped only once in a forest and been allowed to relieve themselves at night. A signal of knocks from the driver's cabin had been arranged to let them know when a border patrol was being approached. Inside the truck there was nowhere they could relieve themselves so someone suggested they make one side of the truck their latrine and all sleep on other side. They dragged some cylinders and boxes across to create a divide but sometimes the urine trickled across to the other side anyway.

The clatter of the truck and passing traffic were something she quickly got used to. Much harder were the heat and thirst as no one had brought enough water for such a long journey. On the third morning, as she imagined it, even over the stench inside the lorry she could smell something different. The smell of brine. Ocean. They had reached the ocean.

Oh, oh! cries Ingénue, when she sees two humpbacks breach, shattering the ocean's glass blue sheen. Where? shouts Cowboy Hat. *How come I never see them and you do*, even when you're driving?

Eagles flank their pathway, swooping down alongside the truck, which levitates above the tarmac's haze. Ingénue rests an arm on the rolled down window. She purses her lips and whistles to the birds, offering them fragments of quesadilla. Cowboy Hat opens one eye. Eagles alight on her lover's arm, snatching morsels from her open hand. I was gonna eat that, mutters Cowboy Hat then goes back to sleep.

Like a jackdaw flapping dark wings her mother swoops down shrieking: Stupid girl, what have you done? Rocío stands surrounded by the broken pieces of the tureen, *caldo* soup running green in different directions across the flagstones. Her mother slaps her so hard she topples over and a shard of terra cotta cuts her bare leg. Soon a red stream trickles across to meet the green one, which now turns browner on its journey between strewn leaves of *col rizada* and diced potatoes. Stopped by a sudden large sprig of *tomillo* it forms a pool until it finds a way to flow round it. Rocío opens and closes her mouth, but no sound comes out. *Who do you think will pay for this. You? Or maybe he will?* her mother carries on shouting. *Shall we ask your dear daddy? Shall we break all the plates just for fun?* If Rocío were a fish she could dive into the blood and soup, swim far away to the ocean where no one would find her.

Rub a finger of lard into your labiolitos to ease the friction, smear the juice of granadas into your pubic hair and down each thigh. It will make him think it's your time of month, the older ones advise Rocio. *Fight back with elbows and teeth, these are your natural weapons. No, don't struggle, don't move a muscle, it only arouses them more.* They can't agree. *Wriggle quicksilver when he relaxes his hold,* baberita mi. *Look,* her aunt points at the sky through the small window, *have the squirrels nested down? Are the geese flying low? Can you see a halo of diamonds around the moon? Pray snow falls tonight and cuts off the mountain pass, then the soldiers won't find us.*

Ian Seed

from New York Hotel

Late

After Joseph Cornell

The palatial hotel is over a century old and retains its grand style. The wooden lift still sits in its steel cage. Leaving my suitcase with the porter, I go upstairs to say hello to my father, who has arrived earlier that day. But there is nobody in his room. I take the ancient lift again and go wandering from floor to floor. The search through ornate corridors is so pleasurable that I soon forget what it is I am looking for. One room has its door open. A woman as glamorous as a silent movie star is lying on the silk sheets of her bed. She blows me a kiss and beckons with her finger. I stand in her doorway, unable to move. Then she sneezes, and I hurry on my way. Eventually I find my father sitting at a table in a lounge on the top floor. He is staring at his watch while waving away a waiter in a white tuxedo. He looks disappointed when he spots me, as if he should have known all along I would only be up to my old tricks again.

Country

I was always hanging around the same place, the Bar Italia, hoping something would come up – a job, an adventure, or a sexual liaison. The barman offered me some medicines he had under the counter. They would never give you these at the chemist's, he said.

He was right. They made me feel better. I went to call my mother from the bar's phone-booth. The English dialling tone started even before I had put in my gettoni; something must have gone wrong with the phone, but this meant I could talk to my mother for free, though I had no idea what it was I was going to say. A queue – or rather, since this was Italy, a small crowd – started to build behind me. There were murmurs of discontent – why was I taking over the only phone in the bar, and one of the very few phones in town? So I had an excuse to hang up.

I went back to my little round table, and sat down to take some more medicine with my *espresso*. But it made me sad that I had not talked to my mother, and I glanced over at the phone booth to see how long I would have to wait before I could call again. To my surprise, the booth was empty. They had not been waiting to use the phone at all. They were simply resentful because I was a foreigner.

An expat friend wandered in. He was in a similar position to me, but older. We spent the whole day together, switching from coffee to red wine in the afternoon. I was more optimistic than he was, but if I'd had any sense I would have taken a long look at my companion and realised what awaited me unless I did something to change my life. He kept loading the same country song over and over again onto the jukebox until the barman told him to stop.

Debts

Back in Paris on business, I paid a surprise visit to my old friend Pierre. I thought he would greet me warmly but he was strangely reserved. It turned out that since his father died, he no longer had any money and was behind with his rent. In my youth his family had been more than generous with me and now he wanted me to return the kindness. Before I could reply, there was a knock on the door. The huge-bellied landlord, with a couple of henchmen at his side, demanded that I pay the arrears. I told him I didn't have that kind of money, but both of us knew it wasn't true. He asked me to meet him later in rue X near the station and to bring along all a suitcase of cash. When I got there, I saw it wasn't a 'rue' at all, but a boulevard, as I pointed out to him, because it consisted of wide lanes on either side of a strip of grass, which was dying, as I also pointed out to him, due to all the traffic fumes.

Rogues

The elephant chased us through the forest. Did it really bear us malice, or was it just curious?

We came to a rock face, impossible to climb. I turned, picked up a log and swung it to scare the elephant away. Instead, it reached its trunk towards us, almost tenderly.

I grabbed my wife's hand. We ducked around the elephant and ran up a hill between close-set trees.

On the other side was a deserted mansion. But now a bunch of locals was after us. Were they cops or criminals?

They were nearly at the door of old dining hall where we were hiding. We climbed up onto a wide, tall cupboard in the corner, convinced we would not be found. Then we heard a ladder being put against the cupboard and a moment later a small torch was shone in our faces. But the torch was held by a woman with a kind face. She looked as if she had discovered two naughty children, rather than a bewildered, middle-aged couple.

Hilda Sheehan

Cabbage is the secret to a view of the future

At night, a plate of cabbage and the vagabond of my dreams appears outside Sainsburys on my walk home from work. Something of the cabbage in him, something of the future too. Should I stop dreaming by refusing the cabbage but this bored me. I needed the future, I needed the vagabond. To give him my loose change made me feel better, daily. On nights without cabbage I slept, I slept without dreaming of a future made of homelessness and a need to give to it. How can I walk past any other unknown vagabond?

Donkey Governments

The donkey it had no legs but there was mud for it and could slide out of roads in the moans of animal cows who walked like he once had and there was mud for it when there were no eyes on this donkey or those eyes we so admired there was mud for it when it's belly sunk and its teeth sunk and its heavy liver sunk there was mud for it when nothing could save the mud or the donkey legs were received in limb-loads awaiting hand-outs empty of giving.

Going Cold

We were called to the bedside of the suicide. Tubes coming out of it in unrecognisable piss and junk. I'd hoped that this might stop it from being hung, slashed or drowned, but I failed. Sitting side by side, we discussed the burger going cold, intended to cheer us up. There was favourite chocolate. 'I have consumed whole packets of capsules intended for you,' said the inconsiderate murderer, waiting in an ear. 'Let's rearrange the furniture into listed negativity, and make sure each pillow is depressed.'

Criminals of Love

'Marriage to me isn't that funny all of the time,' and while hating the idea, she threw kitchen things in his face and he ended up calling the Enthusiastic Police. 'This doesn't mean we are against your marriage,' they handcuffed out-loud, while barricading the freezer to isolate the fish fingers. 'Isn't cold peas enough for you criminals of love?' The shopping list became longer and longer until crumpets scraped the floor, as if in deep need. This was used in evidence when the dirty kitchen itself was brought to justice for having a certain effervescent fun without them.

Alasdair Paterson

My life as a detail

When I fell down in the wood did the trees hear? Did anyone?

How long would I have needed to lie motionless, supine in the wood aforesaid, to be pronounced dead? A minute, a week or a month? A few hundred years? And then, pronounced dead by whom? By you? By an expert? Before or after the leaves cover me? Is there in fact the slightest chance of a single leaf covering me? Do leaves fall here? Am I in fact dead now? What do I mean by 'fact'? What do I mean by 'now'? Is this a deathly pallor or leaf dapple? Or is the paint ageing, changing, though so much more slowly than flesh would?

Shall we go forward on the shared understanding that I really am dead? Shall we assume that understanding is something we can really share? Can we retain the word 'really', with all its dubious, head-scratching applicability, for the time being? What is the time with you, by the way? Am I in time and if so what time?

How do you die in a wood? In my own time, i.e. in the time herein represented? Shall we consider homicide? The footpad stealthy? The cuckold enraged? The war party past caring? The lunatic, terrified and terrible? The family, as usual? Or mishap, perhaps? The tree root? The fallen bough? The passing boar? The lightning strike? Should we not consider natural causes various? The whole unknown mechanism within, shuddering to a standstill, heart, brain, lungs, failing in a wood? Should we not suspect judicial issues or similar? The squeal at the end of the manhunt? Gurgle and twitch till the bough breaks? Is self-harm, alas, a legitimate line of enquiry? What about divine judgement? Does it exist? If so, does it cover all of the above? If not, can I blame the artist?

What do I look like? Is this a good colour? Can we blame the light through the green leaves? Do you agree, it doesn't look good for me? Supine, white hair, eyes staring upward? Can you see me, now?

Who else do you think will see me? The peasant and his horse, perhaps they'll see me next, as they plough a furrow in the direction of the wood? The shepherd who notices nothing, not even his sheep, but might hear a cry of discovery? In a moment? The fisherman distracted by a big ripple? The ships sailing on? Everyone who misses everything, even the tangle of legs and wings and estuary water out there?

You didn't miss that fall, though, did you? The watery one? At least, not the moment of impact? Wasn't it intended you would notice? The title being a clue? The Fall of Icarus? Or maybe Landscape with the the Fall of Icarus? Doesn't that get you looking? And the artistic framing that leads your eye there eventually? The splash you see, that no-one in the picture sees? Being the point about suffering? That no-one sees? But who notices me, here, lying in a wood? Did you really notice? How many times did you look before you noticed? Did you get a tip-off? About looking for the hidden meaning, the same meaning as the splash everyone in the picture misses, but a meaning you missed too? The real meaning? In a blind spot, in the corner of a scene, in a wood?

So will the plough-horse discover me in a second? Will he shy away? Will the proverbs rise like bones from the glistening furrows? The careless shepherd dreams while his sheep stray? The plough doesn't stop just because a man dies? About suffering they were never wrong, the old masters?

My life with the dead white males

As I was motivating up the Cork to Dublin highway, who should I spy but my father-in-law at large among the roadside picnics, big potato thumb extended. I hit the brakes fast—hard enough to make St Christopher on the mirror dance the St Vitus and the parish raffle tickets on the dashboard make a random draw (first prize: a brand-new combine harvester; second prize: the hamburger-van concession by the weeping statue; third prize: a week with the flagellant order of your choice). He climbed in, still with that

Hollywood smile. He said: *How are things in Port Sunlight?* I said: *The Wirral is everything that is the case.* I said: *Jim, we all thought you were dead.* He said: *Only in a manner of speaking.*

As I was swimming with the ease of a young gazelle down the River Mersey, hardly distinguishable from the great grey-green greasy Limpopo apart from Liver Birds snacking on orchids and the flotsam of Stratocasters, my brother at the Pier Head in full military fig (King's African Rifles) proffered his swagger stick to help me out. This was unexpected. Says I: *What's with the uniform then, Davy?* Says he: *I wear it for its proven climatic advantages and for the regimental motto: You Never Drown In The Same River Twice.*

As I was labouring up Arthur's Seat, amusing myself with haiku misshapes like—

> *In a minute*
> *when I get my breath*
> *back, the famous view.*

—my father joined me for the final stretch, tacking between gorse and basalt on a moonless night. The famous view was Edinburgh, our city, like a computer etherised upon a table, lid prised off to reveal that old-time Calvinist binary, *light* or *not light, right* or *very fucking wrong, pal.* He was checking if I'd lost my sense of humour, seeing I'd scattered his ashes here from an extinct volcano and never got the joke. Me: *Things got a bit black there for a while. And I did worry where your ashes might fetch up.* Him: *That was fine, apart from the speck that went into a mutton pie at Raith Rovers. Don't worry, Aly. It's always darkest just before the Scottish Enlightenment. Moreover, a scattering of the ashes will never abolish chance.*

My turn at the oracle business soon enough. I'll try to remember: good intentions, something Delphic. The rest is up to them.

Claire Crowther

A Pacifist Matriarch Finds
Herself at the Royal Air Show

Though they dye cloud red
        with a secondsworth of exhaust,
                I'll rest

while the chief pilot
        calls them to cross each other – *uuppp,*
           haaruupp –

since Two and Four waft
        half a smoke heart each – *formation:*
           python –

or get chips, or veer
        off to buy stickers. Could I break
           and take

this moment, feeling
        no body's weight and surely no bomb's
           falling?

Once More, Undo the Breach

The landlord of my rotting flat has announced he'll renew
every window.
He's inspired.   He's a cathedral builder

of the sort of ecclesiastical architects who decide
three small holes
and an arrow pointing to the light switch

deliver visibility. Yet windows make mighty
shocks in walls.
No glazed room is at ease. Relax, my frames

are metal and that's not reprehensible. Vinyl would be
shortlived as
snow-drops and here he comes. Galanthophile.

Shtummer

Where is the world?
Burly as it is, it sees to ice creams.
She,
small enough to be grabbed as if to be killed,
stilled at least, by me, is held against her
will.
Doesn't the whole human parent hear her *won't*
shout against my tidal *no*? Why am I not
blocked in my turn? Me, who subjugated
her jump onto water-equipped rocks to drown?
I'm left to mourn by-standing. Tense and not free,
shtummed by the bay.

Cathy Dreyer

Migrant c

for Tania Hershman (no 'c')

He thinks you can find
a c, on e it's lost. But you an't
whistle for it, or plu k the lyre
to make it ome ba k. You may
find tra es, in Poland or Gree e,
if you know what to look for,
whi h is halk. halk is made of
 ountless mi ros opi c shells,
subje ted to geologi al eras of seismi
pressure. The shells were se reted
by tiny protozoans whi h lived and
died a hundred million years ago,
and armed themselves with
minis ule al ium arbonate
platelets, or rings, for prote tion,
perhaps from predating
zooplankton. No one is quite sure.
When they died, their shields
fell like snowflakes, dan ing,
through warm, shallow waters,
as though they had all the time
in the world and no spe ial
pla e to be, when they were
always lo ked on target, heading
for the c bed. There, they lay at the
mer y of te toni eruptions and re-
settlements, pressed into ever
 ondensing layers of spa e, pressed
into seams of soft, fossiliferous ro k.
You need a c sometimes. A c to sail
boats on. Boats to Afri a, boats to
Ameri a, boats to Never omingba kia.

56

You read a c, too. Youreadac.
Or You rid a c.
Youridac Youridac Youridac.
Maybe this time he will
trust. Maybe this time
he will ommit to the musi ,
let you find your path through
the shadow lands. Maybe this time
he won't turn around.

Originating

start from here, but here I am, I wouldn't
from here, but here I am, I wouldn't start
here, but here I am, I wouldn't start from

but here I am, I wouldn't start from here,
here I am, I wouldn't start from here, but
I am, I wouldn't start from here but here

am, I wouldn't start from here, but here I

I wouldn't start from here but here I am,

wouldn't start from here, but here I am, I

Isobel Armstrong

The Atheist as Refugee
(Atheist Series, No. 3)

lie at the bottom of the sky
in the bombed street's chasm

a patch of petrol   a smear of blood
on concrete   they left behind

crawl along this space beyond nowhere
the dimness is not light or darkness

there is only thought here but
it does not grow dreams

somebody else's soft warm body
is unimaginable

nothing grows here so I thought to plant
plastic flowers

this must be hell for
death has already been and gone

a single pomegranate seed here
would be voluptuous

what did I hear in the distance? Qui tollis peccata mundi
that takest away the sins of the world...

all nonsense   he lifts them up occasionally
then they fall back   you hear them fall with a crash

words shrivel
plastic flowers shrivel
petrolpatch
bloodsmudge

Carrie Etter

The Gist

These words come from the first page of The White House's "Fact Sheet: What Climate Change Means for Illinois and the Midwest," dated 6 May 2014 and beginning with the word today.

Today, phenomena generated farmers and ranchers vulnerable to late spring freezes.

Today, importantly, Illinois.

Today, the Administration acknowledges climate.

Today, pests consider added stresses.

Today, already, already....

Today, the Obama generated a plan.

Today, climate impacts already underway include increased heat, flooding, drought, late spring freezes, pests, disease, economic shocks, and extreme weather events.

Today, Illinois alter[s] in ways that most people in the region would consider detrimental.

Tokens

For the Victorians a curl of hair in a glass locket represented mourning and memory. Long ago you gave me a plastic envelope of childhood hair. Would I have worn my mother's hair thus, if the mortician hadn't lost the locks I asked for? I should give it back, give it to my successor. From the first months after her death I was eyeing her birthstone in jewelers' windows, till I settled on a white gold ring, a central dark pink stone, minute diamond trim. Your curls lie in my jewelry box; from time to time I open the drawer and they startle me with their honey sheen, their untouchable silk. For a week I thought my work done; I had my memorial and I wore it every day. Why, after all this time, haven't I given the envelope back? I started looking on eBay, bought a ruby pendant, a pair of earrings, another ring, and another ring. Locks or rubies, I hoard my losses.

Future Interlude

The blackouts began as occasional, say one a week, but by the third month, we hoped for two hours of energy every other day. Bathing, laundry, baking and television found their places in a cycle, depending on one's priorities, though no one would say priority: the word was need. And so our needs sharpened and steadily redefined us. Yes, the new electricity exaggerated and undermined our humanity, and some thrived on the change, some wept.

Future Interlude (Kassandraic)

Some called the oracle a noose, and when the oracle became fact, the same people pointed at sea and reckoned it desert, gestured toward sky and groaned water. Some called the oracle a noose and blasphemed it. Some called the oracle a noose and behaved as though they did not feel the rope scratch their necks. One day we refuse to eat the dog caught in the steel-toothed trap, and another day we droop as we wrench its neck. Some called the oracle a noose and led all who followed over the precipice.

Sarah Cave

Reversed Catechism

In this dark wilderness, do we walk?
webs of silken linearity

This is what makes the world dark.

In this dark wilderness, do we seek?
an abandoned home

This is what makes the world dark.

In this dark wilderness, are we tender?
shells broken – warmth, inner cocktail

This is what makes the world dark.

In this dark wilderness, are we obscured?
concealed in rock pools, moon making milk of darkness

This is what makes the world dark.

Downward Melody

Or, **the science of hot air balloons and ice**

We had to create our own world
visible from the air

woolly-mammoth drawn carriages
translucent people

word harnessed by thick furs
mammals stripped to bone

a sideways glimmer of rotting gum
and false optimism

crazed toasting of champagne saved
from the wreck of wicker and sail

a flimsy offering to an ocean that is both
sea and sky

Slava sleeps peacefully as young men perish.

Naming the stone
after Robert Lax

stone
is clear
ing of
mind
slow
deep
voice
makes
horizon
dim-
lit
orison
bear
able

sean burn

heather leigh
(from cracked handful ov blue -on free jazz / free improv musicians)

foot forced to floor
accelerants burn to lair
signalling from stars
the howl life-giving no un-
hinged holler but redeeming

mette rasmussen
(from cracked handful ov blue -on free jazz / free improv musicians)

deliquesce around
mercury badass heels
reel in golden nets
ov air snare times under-tow
and towering play it rare

sabine vogel
(from cracked handful ov blue -on free jazz / free improv musicians)

wings liquid vibrates
wind-funnels - that whispered
tunnelling ov desire
as lungs long lunge blows urgency
over the singing notes

still alone in her voices

still
alone
in her voices

darkflame
jaggering - un
able to still

breath
ever-still
nestling

mindmine
– distill

tha' blade
within
still a child

still in the academy
silence on the ward
book without word

meds jitter
unable
to still

masque
stilling
never-eyes

still
on
her
back
– her
skin

psych
mindstrike
de-stilling

birthing
the unstill
whorled

conspiracies still
outstare the wall

Simon Perchik

Five Poems

*

You fill in the name then prop it
with the same black ink
that will widen for the underline

and keep the word from falling
as your shadow still holding on
to the pen and your fingertips

that stop by twice a day
and each evening draw a name
on wood the way rings in a tree

keep count how many times
you circle her graveside
to keep it from moving, warmed

under a sun made from paper
whose silence goes on living
as just another word for two.

*

It's all they know —these drops
fall, then feed —by instinct
coil around their prey till a puddle

oozes out the ground —rain
will never stop swallowing you dead
though for a few hours at a time

you become water, make your escape
as mist where there was none before
rising the way your tears even now

are burning out between your fingers
as the stench you need for ashes
and forgetfulness —you become a sea

ankle deep, with tides and a shoreline
where something will happen
someone will turn up pulling a boat.

*

The man in the mirror pictures you
covering his forehead with a cap
the way a grave is held in place

by a lid piecing together his grey hairs
makes you lean closer to the glass
—it's a ritual, a tight fit

and though you tilt the brim side to side
the dirt stays blanketed with ice
and every morning now —the man facing you

wants you to close his eyes then sing to him
over and over the same lullaby, help him
remember the darkness, its little by little.

*

The lamp she drank from never dries
is kept on though its glint
still remembers when this cup

was lit by boiling water then darkened
for clouds and the turbulence
when you would reach in, hands on fire

and among the coat hangers a dress
still warm, dangling, slowing down
snared, swallowing the sleeves

—from this light a tide still goes out
as the hot glue keeping the cup open
fastened to every coast, every rim

stained with its emptiness and your mouth
coming back every few hours to touch
where her lips should be.

*

Before paper becomes paper it already knows
a great weight was needed :ink that will drift
into a sea as the silence mourners leave

for bottom stones though you dead
can tell from the stillness a boat is near
were given a ticket the way gas lamps

now line these streets so each grave
is lit, is fastened to the ground
by those footsteps from someone

who offers their hand disguised as a note
asking you to come or let it in as rain, puddles
drenched, dripping from each word and fingertips.

Mark Harris

Entrance to the Dove Holes

(after Joseph Wright of Derby)

Erosions we follow
down limestone pale as

erasure
windblown contour, bone laid bare

to the open oval the eye knows
the way through

hollows wept dry, gray washes
of looped space

winding toward a keyhole of light
the plumb line

unspools, a soft call echoes

Slow Morning

Ghost of sun
a far corner bends

into a right angle
angel

one high pane shines
dust to dust

broken line
the stairwell's

a grayscale down
to dark

things the eye
revises

Amulet

A striding figure
of light, in the dark

turns out to be stone
a god, a man

broken off at
the knees and wrists

blue chalcedony
the scale of

a woman's thumb
gigantic, a faint

fault twisting
through the perfect

torso, so smooth
it must be warm

Changeover

(for Gerrit)

The objects are gone
from the wall case lined

with blue-green silk
faded nearly to white

the silhouettes left
by their long exposure

vivid as the virgin cloth
I remember the man

who placed the things
that shaped these shadows

his hands—at ease now—
trembling with care

Eluned Jones

My English

Llywelyn's death-song ignites, rain re-making
the drabness of my coat into something uncommon.
Gruffudd knew this intensity of a grey autumn;
his words burning centuries, my thoughts fashioned
as leaves as missals as missiles. Now
the old crow elaborates wind into denuded wings,
his call an obsession for the pasty-faced palms
of men who fire borrowed synapses between screen and screen
while coffee mingles with spices on my tongue
as I attempt in an illusory moment
to taste the tang of a decadent chocolate.

Van Eyck's 'Adam'

The pity, tempera and oil on panel.
Texture has become unpronounceable,
blending light with despair; such capture
in the definable moment when knowledge
is brutality and a flawed man in his veins
darkens into the physicality of sudden, palsied
bone, unfathomable muscle – the humble
material of his sweat, of his aware, cringing
sex. Eyes recess; an artist's hands
disturb the outside of mortality – his
translucent sin rendered as if the finger
could encroach this candid density
that foreshortens an unlooking stride.
A son will make death in his discarded blood.

Overrunning Engineering Works

Imagine being able to evangelise an overwrought grapefruit in seconds without having to wait for some grout and eradicate 100s of jam jars. Not an eyebrowed instrumentalist, just you. With Overrunning Engineering Works you can – simply text message the penguin to be tiled, apply a horoscope and that's it; you have a long-lasting catastrophe in seconds – it's as simple as that. Formulated in tall hats and used by respected heatstore radiators, it's great for renovating goldfish, supermarket two-for-one offers or any instruction manuals where common sense has been seeping through. It can also be used as an excuse for seagulls or General Elections, before treating with marmalade. Keep a born-again hatstand beside every overenthusiastic trumpet player and enjoy the next little emergency. Long term adjectives can cost hundreds of pounds to put right; don't let that Saturday night television damage your slippers – put it right now with Overrunning Engineering Works.

Rachel Sills

from Essays on Rain

On the Edge of a Roof a Cloud Is Dancing

Threat of rain. It's slate grey today across the way but I do like an urban landscape, lovely lead-lined ranges. I have used up all my data and I and I want to call a taxi due to peep-toe shoes. Those grim hooves. Them grim hooves. Rain tap-dancing across the roofs.

The Evening Cuts a Fine Figure in the Theatre of Roofs

Rain that moistens the moss on the roofs of the lofts of Castlefield. From a tram through these roofscapes, a seat in the gods, the seat of the gods, you see little lives play out. Someone owns a book called The Breathing Book. It's me. If I could see, I'd consult it. I'm concerned. But in this weather I just stroke the blurred line of figures.

Under the Weight of Clouds

Rain like a cow relieving itself and I mean that most sincerely. Afterwards, roses lie battered in the manner of a disillusioned new wife. I can no longer look at things, the sky is so heavy. This contains scenes which may be upsetting to some viewers. Tiny apples have been massacred in the June drop and lie in pools of russet light.

The Sky Is Darker Along the Rooftops

Severe localized downpour. A furious nomad of a cloud settles over Whalley Range. Whalley Range responds in kind. It is often furious; something is brewing behind the windows. Brace yourself. Raindrops like broad beans, like bullets, like a boy bombarding a bathtub with ballbearings.

The Scythe of the Rainbow, Broken Behind the Clouds

Soft weather. I am bending over backwards, baby. The street is like watercolours though, like the outskirts of Paris and nothing can be vicious today - all the edges are rubbed off. I'm going to wear a trenchcoat and you can guess what's underneath. The sky is ajar behind clouds that are scoops of lead.

The Diamond-Shapes of the Roofs

Drizzle in a steady march of verticals. Tonight Matthew I'm going to be Joan Collins in a fur coat. The dazzle on the windowpane. I want to throw off this head, and watch it burn up and frazzle in the puddles. I'm sizzling, my poor migrainous temples are lit with fires. Through the curtain of drizzle the spectacle of shapes, the kaleidoscope of roofs fizzing and turning in a flash of strokes and figures.

On Every Slate Sliding from the Roof Someone Had written a Poem

It's raining up. Smells of meat, but this requires the purity of nettle tea and greenery. The tinkly tinkly tune of *Greensleeves*. The drug dealer arrives in his ice-cream van and a queue forms. The air is pungent like ozone and weed and indeed there is a dripping from leaves and trees and a rhythmic running from roofs.

Agatha Abu Shehab

The Scrying Mirror

Lightning, Sand and Silver
bound together in a violent marriage;
these are the materials of magic,
these are the materials of Mirrors.
Be wise if you offer your thoughts
to reflection. You stand before the *other* plane,
sly, with a neat trim of faux gold or flashing bulbs.
You stand before the twin of everything. Sly
and aloof whilst envisioning your fate.
Never flickering, never altering its gaze on now
as you graze your chin with a fingertip –
bothering a blemish. Now, as you embrace
your beauty, now, as you abandon it. Now
as you bargain with the glass.

After Me

Scalding hot water will frost
before your eyes from every spout
in your house. Birds will fly
at your windows . Your evening
TV show will fuzz with white noise,
a non-human voice will speak,
you'll be sorry for loving a selfish poet.
I have spun silk
out of my abdomen spinners
around you.
I have dug deep mines
into you and plundered
your precious metals.
After me, you might sense
six phantom arms
you cannot see or touch
tingling and itching
six times over.
After me, flies
might drop at your feet
like ripe berries.
Did you know
my love, that a Spider's web
is five times stronger than steel?

Valentino Gianuzzi

Three Erasures from César Vallejo's *Trilce*

Between 2004 and 2007, the Irish poet Michael Smith and I collaborated in a translation of César Vallejo's poetry, eventually brought together in one volume in 2012 as *The Complete Poems*. During those years Michael lived in Dublin and I lived in Lima and our translation was done through email correspondence: it was an intense exchange of almost daily messages with attached drafts of versions, discussions about word choices and arguments about how to read Vallejo's famously cryptic poems.

Although I started living in London in 2009, I never met Michael personally. Peruvians need a separate visa to travel to Ireland and I focused on my studies with the hope that, after finishing my PhD, I would find the time to travel more extensively and meet Michael. His death in November 2014 left that hope unfulfilled.

As an attempt to try to approach this void textually, I began to work on erasing words from our translation of *Trilce*. That erasure seemed to me to best represent that 'falta sin fondo' (to use Vallejo's words) caused by Michael's parting. I have approached the act of erasure not with a set of pre-conceived constraints or restrictions, but with the freedom that Vallejo's work embodies. At times, it seemed to me that Vallejo's original words should be transplanted into the erased English translation, in order for the result to foreground more clearly the palimpsest-like qualities of this mode of writing. Below is a sample of this work.

I

        that din,

let

    it   be late,
            be better
    , the simple
   briny
  insular

swish.

the liquid   evening
    THE PROUDEST

        unafraid,
the deadly line of balance

||

   Time

              drains
time

   Era

           en vano.
   el claro día
      era

     Mañana.

El   caliente

             mañana.

   Name

     that which
        suffers
name   mE.

III

        time

            is ringing
               dark.

    Mother

keep
tolling
twanging

              still

      stay
Mother

         be
    the
                 day
without
          the pond

            be
                  the
              first
     they leave   at home

             away.

I'm   the dark
   hope
             here.

Jon Thompson

from The Notebook of Last Things

Shadow calligraphy wavering on the ground.
Slender branches write Chinese characters
over one another.

*

The play of afternoon light & tree shadow
on green grass should
be remembered for its ever-changing grace.

*

Old shotgun houses built
by former slaves torn down &
replaced by white McMansions.

————————

Things get lost in
words, generations
lost without a trace.

*

Things get lost in
words & no escaping it, we
need/want/desire that loss.

*

Death, it's said, is not
a thing. It's just you
happening in time.

_____

Screeching of the Norfolk
Southern wheels coming to a halt,
hauling chemicals west.

*

The poet who crossed
the street couldn't
see the poem in front of him.

*

Through the years he remembered
the dream of a teenager friend, a suicide, sitting
in the branches of a tree saying something unheard.

_____

The Recording Angel does not
listen to the arguments regarding why the innocents
are gunned down. He just tallies the numbers.

*

Other countries have poets
with dangerous dreams. We have
zealots & businessmen.

*

"Language should be tortured to tell
the truth." The Recording Angel notes,
indifferently, the need, & the lies.

———————

At the Gringo-a-Go-Go
talk of Chile & Peru & the Cuban café next
door, now doing Cuban & Argentinian food.

*

Table umbrellas extended red
against the sun. The restaurant: a converted
gas station. Traffic noise eddies around tables.

*

A man in dirty stinking clothes totters
in traffic. I saw that man earlier,
lounging on the sidewalk.

———————

Memorial garden for the teacher slain
by her husband at the local elementary school bordered
by flowers & a periwinkle bench for reflection, but no plaque.

*

At the university built by slaves
they just renamed a building named for a
Reconstruction-era KKK leader.

*

Violinist for the symphony seen
cycling with a wounded violin
to the violin repair shop.

_____

The wondrous game that power plays
with all things. A perfected fear builds
a wall of hate, trapping those in & out.

*

What is the true name of power?
The true name of the powerful:
the true name of the powerless.

*

Let us be clear. Let us be
clear. The horizon is the horizon
against which we will be measured.

James Sutherland-Smith

3 poems from The River and the Black Cat

*

The grammars of all our friends
have gathered on the powerlines
and the topmost twigs of trees
then ascended to inscribe
on the past or the future
various loudly twittering
four-dimensional figures,
a murmuration of syntax,
tachyons and tachyoffs,
nobody will see us coming
when we're gone and do be quick
into an ether where we've barely.
Tachyderms lift their long
hairy snouts from swamps to trumpet
the coming apocalypse.
The river suffers tachycardia
when swollen with rain water.
Tachyscopes provide no other
finding than infinity
ends neither sooner nor later.
Tachydramas are enacted
on pavements in our neighbourhood,
a couple shouting at each other
in dialect about stains
of bodily fluids on knickers
which belong to neither of them.
The black cat becomes a grin
a mile high which a gothic church
could never accommodate.
You and I interlocute
then interlock and can't be

told apart of life's simple pains
and pleasures oneself whilst
reading the inside pages
of the Daily Telegraph
featuring an especially
scandalous divorce's details
the assassin to leave no phrase
alive or identifiable
after forensic examination.

*

The black cat knows all there is to know about
the four hundred thousand years before the Big Bang.
It's a pity she's so far outside language.
You've never played the violin for me.
Just the once I overhear your showing
our granddaughter a scrap of Vivaldi.
Olga! I think , but then take a linguistic turn
for the better away from ranting on the radio
and recall Toni Gramsci in pain all his life
as the black cat comes in out of the rain
and grooms her fur which settles under the forces
of gravity and a tongue with hooks
into its petty bourgeois order and shine.
Rain punctures the river surface with silvery glints,
a long cadenza of whispers and light.

*

It's time for beautiful disintegrations.
Colours splinter becoming motes
in the eyes of their beholders.
Louie is noting the family resemblances
of different flowers: a rose
is a lily is a chrysanthemum

is my language game.
Fred is tending to the horses
of instruction in my words.
It's pointless to ask if they exist elsewhere
when elsewhere is always here.
The river is a hyphen seeking
to join the empire of the senses
to the republic of letters.
The black cat is playing inside its own
extra-linguistic reality
if she but knew it though the disadvantage
of such self-knowledge doesn't burden a cat.
You and I put our arms around each other
and these absences of true stories and hug.
We're long past living in kingdoms of gold,
silver, bronze and iron. Instead we flicker
between screens of a world enabled
by a trace element mined by child labour
in the catchment area of the Upper Congo.

Lucy Sheerman

from One-Way Chorus

i.

You have a one way ticket
There is something soothing about this
It could be joyous and amazing
It would be nice to be somewhere with no distractions
You don't have to think
Just listen to all the crackle of life
You have a very curious nature
You can't ignore the clutter
Don't grow accustomed to it
In the end you won't have to accept it

Could you make a decision like that?
All sorts of things could go wrong
You can't be what you don't know
I don't think you have to say yes
Don't take the risk without knowing
Would it make you stronger?
Could you become a much more global person?
Could you do without books?
The scary bit only lasts three minutes
Subliminally it sounds like you want me to take the risk

ii.

We are in a long distance relationship
To have just the one other makes it a challenge
Do we agree on anything?
I'd like to continue my life with you
Shared experience brings you closer
If I had to go with someone I'd prefer to go with you
Perhaps we feel we ought to want to go
I wouldn't go to live on a desert island with just you

89

You think we'd grow apart
You don't know do you?

Why on earth did we get together?
We don't actually agree on anything
We will get more set in our ways
We might end up counting the days
You spend a lot of your life in a relationship
You live separate but linked existences
Our views are very different
It would be a shock to be talking to each other
We could disagree in order to arrive at an ok outcome
Talk more about bigger issues

iii.
The journey's part of the experience
Who wouldn't want to go?
You really want to know the person you are travelling with
It is just the two of you forever and ever
Maybe it is all one way
We are sharing time together
We are doing something although it might not feel like it
This is a different scenario
Space makes you feel so insignificant
You can think about things in more holistic ways

Every now and then you do fight back
You know who's in charge
Who's going to be the leader?
Dissect how you arrived at that point
You can't always have your own way can you?
You're making yourself vulnerable
The need for other people is there
We could procreate. Create people around us.
We can work together
We might both arrive at the same ending

Robin Fulton Macpherson

The Lakes Have Their Say

White Swedish nights staring at me,
relentless lakes with just one word
they can never stop repeating:
if that word "defied translation"
it might tire of following me
but no,
it's at home in any language.

Evolutionary

Low on the scale? No fins, no feet?
But aspens and jack pines far north
survive
as if there'd been no forest fires,
tormentil tiny and local
survives
as if there'd been no winter ice –
and trailing nasturtium tendrils
reach out the way theologians
reach out hoping to taste the air
beyond the wires of their reason.

Non-Tree

Gone. Nothing left to visit
but a stubborn emptiness
Lombardy Poplar in shape,
the shape as wedged in the air
as a cuneiform sign chipped
in stone, meant to last, lasting.

Lombardy Poplar Revisited

I've carried
a weightless version of that poplar,
in my head,
for years, across the North Sea and back.

In the tree
with a life-sentence in Yorkshire earth
no envy
of the one that seems to defy bounds.

In the tree
with no roots that could hold it in place
no envy
of the one that seems to have a home.

Kjell Espmark

translated by Robin Fulton Macpherson

The Bird-Sermon

I'm all that's left of our village,
too withered to be raped.
They call me feeble-minded
for I claim to know what the birds say
and feel the pain of Africa in my joints.

I've heard the thrushes preaching
on the avaricious rule of the whites
who stroked out a piece of *Genesis*
and left nature gasping
as if unable to breathe.

And I've heard the swallows prophesy
about the black people who'd come
on wings stolen from the *Koran*
and steal our children. The horrified trees
tried to pull up their roots and run.

The rebels hammered us with their message
and forced our girls up onto the lorries –
then I heard the very ground screaming
instead of the murdered victims.

I trudge away in search of my own
in village beyond village,
beyond time if need be.
I see how the forest around me
has retreated to long ago. And the birds seem
as if they've just flown up from Mother Sea.
Their space too is incomplete.

Inquisitio

When my gay leanings were revealed
I was summoned before the inquisition –
ancient men who bowed to each other
in the Spanish fashion
before letting their bodies take shape
from the experienced chairs they sank into.
Their faces were of dark parchment
which had been scraped and scraped
for each century's new text
while preserving traces of the earlier.

Well, did I acknowledge my name, Alan Turing,
and my address in The Right City?
I have never denied my identity.

Before the judges stood a pair of scales.
My war effort was laid in the one pan,
how I cracked the German code
and sketched out a machine
to compete with the human brain.
That I made love with men was laid in the other.
And that scale-pan sank with such force
that the first tipped out its contents.

I was sentenced to have my lips sewn
and my testicles burnt to ash
to prevent my heretical notions
and my diseased seed
from infecting future centuries.

But they failed to erase entirely
that sketch which bore my name.
You who find each other in cyberspace
borrow my voice.

Chorus (2)

Dies irae is upon us
and the century has begun to dissolve in ash.
We had of course expected the spurned god
to rasp earth with his blaze,
but not our own wrath
to turn against us.

Cannae, Waterloo and Verdun
are cursing remnants
of ribs and vertebrae that never disappoint.
And wagging jaw-bones demand revenge.
Wrath gives strength to the jerking bone-splinters,
urges shin-bones and knuckles to pull together.
We've waited long for the signal
that Law has resigned
so once more anything goes.

And now, at the bray of the Assyrian trumpet
we, the dead, rise, rattling.
Awry skeletons dizzy and stumbling
try to make helmets perch on skulls.
We can't wait to pounce on the others' throats,
throats that the last war bit off,
and rip out the hearts of the others,
hearts that have been loam for centuries.
But first we must kill the waverers among us,
those who recognise their anxiety
in the enemy's empty eye-sockets.
Then we can reduce to ash the cities –
which have already been ash for ages.
And it's both now
and a thousand years ago.

Examination

So I'm a "type" that aroused interest
in the Institute for Racial Biology,
and can be read between the lines of the report,
"Partly Lapp-cross types, Espnäs."
In a photo father's cousin Karl-Erik
stands with his brothers Per and Jöns Herbert
in Sunday best, help needed with the cravat.
Arms and legs are embarrassingly short
and the jacket cloth tight round the buttons
from anxiety before the test.
Are the trouser-creases Aryan enough?
The brothers pose on straw in the barn
against a white-washed wall
hinting at extermination
and gaze solemnly into our age.
It's 1931
and history is about to take a long step back.

Father is standing outside the picture
posthumously aghast
at his suddenly impure racial features.

I'm shaken by the diagnosis as such,
an insect fixed in race-biologist
Herman Lundborg's magnifying glass.
The blinking steely-blue eye
on the other side of the lens wonders
if I should be shoved back into the Lapp tent
or set free into the next chapter
of the Thousand Year Plan.

Father's cousins stand at attention still
while the photo ages round them.
They're waiting for the Institute's decision.
As if just unloaded onto the platform.

Mercedes Cebrían

translated by Terence Dooley

Andorra: See what happens

People sometimes mock
little things and Andorra
too is little.
   (300 cigarillos
are no small thing: arranged
in indian file they can cover
up to 27 yards, and what about
two and a half kilos of white
powdered milk
    representing the concept
 of a vast ski-slope.)

Verifiable data, and if we haven't
mentioned the co-princes it's because
we can't get our minds around them, we haven't
brushed their cheeks with our lips, but we do
understand their flag: look, let's fix our eyes
on its 3 primary colours, you could
combine them to make
purple, green or orange with the greatest
of ease, and this probably arouses
dread in us.

What to make of the muddle, of the purchase
of video-cameras in a mountainous
landscape, with freshwater
waterfalls. What to make of
the cataract, the transaction,
the miniature life-blood
flowing through Andorra
whether the shops
are open or not.

As if we were

blind children they described the paintings
in the Prado to us: a princess on the left, the Duke
of Orleans on the right, and us, stock-still,
in front: we looked like anchors
waiting for their respective boats. We lacked
propulsion, the message of the taxi-meter
when it starts ticking: don't even think of
stopping it, if just looking at it makes us feel
we're in motion.

Transport is excellent here (it goes on wheels,
the wheel invented 5000 years ago), but it won't
get us very far. Very far away
are parents in shorts, or a shop
 supplying flat-pack furniture.
                        Then there's the matter of
the glass upside-down: it skates if we place
our fingers on the Ouija board and it's from the far ends
of that skid that our mother-in-laws
or our own children speak to us: the eldest
plays rugby for the university and pronounces it
ragbi, not ruby, like us.   I turn my back on him
and he forgets his Spanish: it's only if we sit down
together in the living-room he uses words like
antediluvian or slough.
        And what can I do about it
if my younger son lives on doughnuts. Doughnuts
were invented 5000 years ago, which explains
why they look like wheels. What use is it, what
do I gain by knowing the ingredients
of wheels and doughnuts.
I learnt the rules of rugby, it didn't
stop my son spraining his right shoulder.

Now that our illiterates are dying
and with them their indestructible

smell, it seems to us the breeze
is trying to explain something. Fear
has melted and it's easier to dry it away
with a rag. Foreigners don't even notice:
this gallery is as crowded as thirty years ago. We
            —and this is a new development –
no longer bark our shins on learning,
with its air of an athlete about to land
on the wrong foot.
All this time had been simple description and yet,
two trains leaving Pontevedra and Burgos
at the same instant and at 90 kilometres an hour
still finally passed each other by. Isn't that
amazing? Doesn't it surprise us just as much
as when that little peep-hole opened up
in the vast boredom? Discovering it is like
talking to daylight, as one friend to another,
standing on a corner. Here is where we learnt about
efficiency and darkness. If we're asked to take part
in a survey in the street, we can answer,
            fearlessly,
twice a month.

Mario Martín Gijón

translated by Terence Dooley

Untitled

I am a withered plant without
the wise juice of your kiss
my fingers broken stems without
the whisper of your s(y/i)n–
copated skin
                        depr(i/a)ved
within these sheets

burnt offering

terrified by terrain untrodden
by you I
wandered through the suburbs
of your name

the irate air
bore embers of scorched pain
weak I sacrificed
on the altar
of your absence
                        from heaven

in propitiation?

missed calls

the prisons are scattered when
stubborn unpredictable your
memory lives on
wherever lost birds
land, flourishing
your codes and signs

walking, waiting

wooden gaze
hard splintered
flitting
over wheels of cars
none
with your licence-plate

in the houseless house

disdain of days in
the robbed throbbing
of night desiring
            you
down yielding
            palpitating
paths and stairs
            where
you were   it is
ploughing the deserted
summer of your stay
the borderless state our
            kingdom
            gone away

Mariangela Gualtieri

translated by Anthony Molino & Cristina Viti

Three Poems

*

Wash your dead. Lose not
the treasured day when
that dear body of theirs is a map
of a land beyond the sea. Slowly, slowly
wash the stiffened dead
the uninhabited shell, cold and empty.
Sense how they unfold – outspread –
more alive now – than when they were living –
released. It is then that the hard oyster
of the dead opens.

*

Mother was a huge ark
I floated in the breath
when my time
would kick
to begin.

Mother was a strong boat
in whom I navigated asleep
burdened with my name and address
and an earthly dream.

Mother was my home then
a hut, a shell, an enormous walnut
of milk. A country where

I curled up. Silent
in focused anticipation
of that scream, that cry
when the room explodes
for a voice that didn't exist
and now is mine.

(translated by Anthony Molino)

*

To the Spring: An Enquiry with Dangerous End-rhyme

So if they weren't there, back then
– the flowers I mean, fifty million years back:
what wanting heart
spilling over with want
what most playful mind
burst forth from its own centre
in colourful fragments of self
its own thinking self.
What heart & what mind
sizzled forth
the law of the blossoming
the colours & forms
& such delicate shading
there where the petals are joined
to the corolla.
What heart, full laden
with a joy we can barely guess at
what acrobat mind
cast into the mire the first handful
& made petal
pistil corolla & the love howl
of the colourful flower?

(translated by Cristina Viti)

Notes on Contributors

AGATHA ABU SHEHAB is British-born, with a degree in Creative Writing from Bath Spa University, and currently lives in Jordan.

ISOBEL ARMSTRONG has appeared *Shearsman* on several occasions. Her poetry features in the women's poetry anthology, *Infinite Difference* (ed. Carrie Etter, Shearsman Books, 2010). Professor Emeritus of Birkbeck, University of London, her academic speciality is Victorian literature.

MICHAEL AYRES has published three collections, including *Kinetic* (Shearsman Books, 2008). He lives in Cambridge.

KEN BOLTON lives in Adelaide. His *Selected Poems 1975-2010* (2012) is still available from Shearsman Books.

SEAN BURN lives in Newcastle-upon-Tyne. His most recent collection, *is that a bruise or a tattoo?* appeared from Shearsman Books in 2013.

SARAH CAVE lives in a wood near Bodmin Moor. She writes poetry, prose and non-fiction and has been published in numerous magazines including *Stride, Osiris, The Clearing* and *Tears in the Fence*. The poems presented here are from a long sequence about a Russian Orthodox monk living on a remote Siberian archipelago. Sarah's debut pamphlet, *Cast on Ice*, was published in May 2016 by Smallminded books, using more poems from the sequence.

MERCEDES CEBRÍAN is a Spanish novelist, journalist and poet. She has also translated a number of volumes from French and English. Her most recent book is a novel, *El genuino sabor* (Random House, Barcelona, 2014).

STUART COOKE is a poet and critic based on Australia's Gold Coast, where he lectures in literary studies and creative writing at Griffith University. His next collection of poems, *Opera*, is forthcoming from Five Islands Press.

TOM COWIN lives in Sussex, and has poems in a recent edition of *Tears in the Fence*. This is his first appearance in *Shearsman*.

CLAIRE CROWTHER lives in Frome, Somerset. She has three collections with Shearsman Books, as well as a recent chapbook, *Bare George* (2016)

TERENCE DOOLEY's translation of Eduardo Moga's *Selected Poems* will be published by Shearsman Books in 2017. His pamphlet, *The Why of It* is published by Argent Press in autumn 2016, and he has edited Penelope Fitzgerald's essays, *A House of Air*, as well as her letters, *So I Have Thought of You*.

CATHY DREYER is currently studying for an M.Phil in Writing under Philip Gross at the University of South Wales.

KJELL ESPMARK (b.1930) was Professor of Comparative Literature at Stockholm University from 1978–1995 and has been a member of The Swedish Academy since 1981, serving as Chairman of The Nobel Committee from 1988 to 2004. He has published over 50 books, and has received many awards, both Swedish and international. In English, three recent collections are available, from Marick Press, Grosse Point, MI— *Lend Me Your Voice* (2011), *Outside the Calendar* (2012) and *The Inner Space* (2014)—all translated by Robin Fulton Macpherson and the author, who have also now prepared a fuller selected poems for publication.

CARRIE ETTER teaches at the Bath Spa University. Shearsman Books publishes her collection *Divining for Starters* and the chapbook, *Scar*, as well as her anthology of women poets, *Infinite Difference*. Seren publishes her most recent full collection, *Imagined Sons* (2014).

MICHAEL FARRELL lives in Melbourne; his most recent collection, *Cocky's Joy*, was published in Sydney by Giramondo in 2015.

ROBIN FULTON MACPHERSON lives in Stavanger, Norway, retired after many years teaching at the local university. *A Northern Habitat. Collected Poems 1960-2010* appeared from Marick Press (Grosse Point, MI) in 2013.

VALENTINO GIANUZZI is Peruvian and teaches at the University of Manchester. His co-translations (with Michael Smith) of the complete poetry of César Vallejo are still available from Shearsman Books.

MARK GOODWIN has three collections and a chapbook with Shearsman Books, most recently *House At Out* (2015).

MARIANGELA GUALTIERI trained as an architect, and founded, with Cesare Ronconi, Italy's famed Teatro Valdoca, for which she currently serves as dramaturge. Widely regarded as one of the more striking and original voices in Italian poetry, her recent publications include the award-winning *Bestia di gioia* (Einaudi, (2010), and *Le giovani parole* (Einaudi 2015).

MARK HARRIS is proprietor of Ornithopter Press, a small publisher of chapbooks by contemporary poets such as John Martone and Joseph Massey. He lives and works in Princeton, New Jersey.

MARIA JASTRZĘBSKA was born in Warsaw and came to England as a child. Her most recent full length collection is *At The Library of Memories* (Waterloo Press, 2013).

ELUNED JONES lives in Aberystwyth, where she is a member of the Word Distillery group, based at the local Arts Centre. Her poetry has appeared in a number of British magazines.

JILL JONES is an Australian poet who has published a number of books, mostly in Australia. Her most recent are *The Beautiful Anxiety* (Puncher & Wattmann, 2014) and *Breaking the Days* (Whitmore Press, 2015).

Julie Maclean is originally from Bristol, but now lives in Australia. Her third collection *Kiss of the Viking* (Poetry Salzburg) was published in 2014. A collaborative pamphlet with Terry Quinn, *To Have To Follow*, appeared in August. Her work appears in *Poetry* (Chicago) and *The Best Australian Poetry*.

Sheila Mannix is based in Cork, Ireland, and has been published in the UK in *Stride* magazine and *Tears in the Fence* and in the USA most recently in *Tripwire: a journal of poetics*.

Mario Martín Gijón taught Spanish Language and Literature at the universities of Marburg (Germany) and Brno (Czech Republic) from 2004 to 2009. An essayist and poet, his most recent poetry collections are *Latidos y desplantes* (2011), *Rendición* (2013) and *Tratado de entrañeza* (2014).

Anthony Molino is a widely published psychoanalyst, Ph.D. anthropologist and literary translator. Born in Philadelphia, he now lives in Italy. His ten books of translations include works by poets Antonio Porta, Valerio Magrelli and Lucio Mariani. His most recent book-length publication is Lucio Mariani's *Traces of Time* (Open Letter Books, 2015).

Alasdair Paterson lives in Exeter and is the author of two Shearsman collections, most recently *Elsewhere or Thereabouts* (2014).

Simon Perchik has been publishing with *Shearsman* since its very first issue in 1981. The author of many books, including a substantial collected edition (*Hands Collected*) from Pavement Saw Press, he lives on Long Island, NY.

Ian Seed has three collections from Shearsman Books, the most recent of which is *Identity Papers* (2016). He teaches at the University of Cumbria.

Hilda Sheehan's first collection, *The Night My Sister Went to Hollywood*, was published by Cultured Llama in 2013. She also won the Poetry Can award for her "contribution to poetry development" in 2013.

Lucy Sheerman lives in Cambridge and is the Chief Executive of the John Clare Cottage Trust and an artist-in-residence at Metal, Peterborough. She is the author of *Rarefied (falling without landing)* from Oystercatcher Press.

Rachel Sills has published the chapbooks, *Two Hundred Houses* (Knives, Forks and Spoons Press, 2015) and *Endless/Nameless*, co-authored with Richard Barrett (Red Ceilings Press, 2014). She is co-organiser of the Manchester-based reading series *Peter Barlow's Cigarette*, and has a PhD on the poetry of Frank O'Hara.

James Sutherland-Smith lives in Slovakia. His most recent collection is *Mouth* (Shearsman Books, 2014).

Jon Thompson teaches at the University of North Carolina, and edits both *Free Verse* magazine and Parlor Press. Shearsman Books publishes his collections *Landscape with Light* (2014) and *Strange Country* (2016), as well as the volume of essays, *After Paradise* (2009).

CRISTINA VITI is a poet and translator based in London. Her translation of Gëzim Hajdari's *Stigmata* was published by Shearsman Books in 2016.